I Love You More

brandon deem

I Love You More

Copyright © 2023 Brandon Deem

Formatting Completed By
Violet Lee Xuan Yin

Book Printed By
Amazon Kindle Direct Publishing

First Printing, 2023

www.ChooseU.org

Letter To The Reader

Dear Reader,

We meet again on book three and with this book I wanted to journey through life's most unpredictable yet awfully beautiful emotions. *I Love You More* is an exploration of self-love, longing, meaning, and romance. This book will help you look forward, backward and most importantly inward, to the scariest, yet hopeful human experience – love. With this book, I wanted to capture what is both raw and relatable to you, the reader. Whether it's the first glance at new love or a trip back to aged love, I hope the words you read warm you like a tight hug.

Sincerely,
B

PS: I Love You More

Our time here on earth
is limited, so if I do
not tell you enough let
this be a forever
reminder that I love
you more

Make home within yourself,
that way no matter
who stays,
who leaves,
or the places you go...
you will always be *home*

Hey,
I am in love with you, yeah you.
With a cracked heart you still find a way to
love endlessly, and I think you're the bravest
person for it.
You cry in tender moments from the pages
you read in those books.
Your heart aches when you see those less
fortunate than you
And I'm starting to question how anyone
could not love a person like you.
I ask that you stay soft, and never let the
weight of the world make you hard.

I
hope
you
never
get
the
smell
of
me
off
your
hoodies
or
the
taste
of
me
off
your
lips

I fall asleep next to you
every night,
only to wake up a little
more in love with you
every day

She is not just my 2AM thoughts when I can't sleep. She's my 6 AM dance in the shower as I wake up, she's my 7 PM when I'm cooking dinner in the kitchen and my 10PM drinks with friends at the bar. She is always on my mind, and I don't want her to ever leave there.

Come, let us get lost in
Paris kissing under the
moonlight sipping wine
from the bottle

Silly of me to never
notice that rooms were
made bright because of you

today i must apologize to myself
for i lost my voice screaming your name
from a thousand rooftops
just to let the world know
you're mine

I'd walk this earth backwards
time and time again
to show you I love you

Sincerely, your best friend

Fall in love.
It doesn't have to be
with a specific
person, for there are
so many things to love.

Fall in love with rainy
days, art museums,
campfires under
starry skies, the smell
of a new book, the
silence, friends who
make you laugh until
you cry.

Fall in love with the
way these things
make you feel, fall in
love with being alive.

this is a reminder that i am human,
i get angry, sad, annoyed
and everything else
but no matter which version i find
myself at,
you accept me every time.

i just wanted to say *thank you*

growing up
i was told 99%
of the people you meet
in your life are temporary,
so i'm kindly asking
you to be my 1%

i took a polaroid picture
of you today.
i took it because
in a world full of people
striving to be a copy of each other,
you are never afraid
to be completely
and utterly yourself
and i'll keep this photo with me
forever

Angels have to exist
because I have no
other way of
describing your
presence in my life

You have the kind of lips

I want to kiss for **eternity**

tonight,
i need you to hold me,
even if it's only because you're lonely.

Please excuse me while I remove all
batteries from every clock
just to be stuck in this moment
with you a little bit longer.

I wanted

my hands

to touch you

in ways your body

has never

been touched

I was born to love you,
convince me otherwise

And that's how you know
you loved them, because
your heart aches, your
stomach drops, and your
lungs cave in, all because
you thought of them being
with someone else

there are people you meet
and in that moment,
you just know you won't
be able to forget them.
They slowly burrow
their way into your atoms.
you are that for me
and it does not matter
which universe I find
myself in,
i would find you in all of
them and i would love you
in every single one

So, what if I told you I loved you.
Actually love you, not just the idea of you.
What if I love the way you tuck your hair
behind your ears constantly when it falls
gently in your face?
What if I love the way you wiggle to get
into your jeans?
What if I love the way you fall asleep,
gentle at first and then all at once.
What if I love you for all that you are and
all that you will be.
Would you say it back?

I MEMORIZED YOUR FACE
AND THE TASTE OF
YOUR SUN KISSED SKIN

I find you
in everything,
in the sky full of stars,
in early morning sunrises
& late-night sunsets,
on rainy Sundays
and every smile I see,
I find you.

So i'll write about you

in each of my poems,

so even when you're gone,

you'll live

forever

They always say to
follow your heart, and
I guess that's why I
always end up back
here with you.

they say you can be anything you dream of…

…so I dreamed of being yours

Take trains by yourself to places you have never been. Fall asleep under the stars alone. Learn to drive a stick shift and then drive so far that you're no longer afraid of not coming back. Say no when it doesn't feel right in your heart, say yes when it does even if those around you disagree. Decide whether you want to be liked or admired and if fitting in is more important than finding out where you path leads.

And if I could,
i'd empty all of me
just so I could be filled
with you

I knew all of her.
My hands knew her touch even
with my eyes closed.
My ears knew her laughter in a
crowded room
My lips knew the taste of her under
white sheets on a messy bed.

You —

are the greatest part of any sunset

ALL
THE
LOVE
I
HAVE
IN
MY
FRAGILE
BEATING
HEART
I
GIVE
TO
YOU

*My heart won't shut up about you
and I'm starting to understand why*

Home is my place in between your embrace,
It's in the seconds between the gentle kisses
It's in the comfort of you saying
"everything will be okay"
Its tucked away in all these beautiful moments
Home is when I lose myself in you

I hope that someday, somebody takes you by the hand just to hold you in their arms and dance. They don't try to pull away or kiss you, they just dance for twenty minutes straight and that's all they do. I hope it happens in the middle of the road, in your living room, in the center of time square, or anywhere. I hope they wrap you up in their arms without any ounce of selfishness in it because you deserve those moments.

I followed my thoughts
until I found peace
I followed my fears
until I conquered them
I followed the sun
until I found warmth
I followed my heart
until I found you

He kissed her forehead
and instantly she knew
to be homesick for a person
is a real thing to.

you deserve a love
that feels like summer

in a world
where it feels like
there are a million things to do,
nothing feels as important
as being right here with you

I've been struggling to understands things inside myself. I don't know how they got there, and I don't know why they're there. But what I do know is that whenever you're around my problems seem so small.

for a second
the world stopped spinning,
the stars exploded in supernova,
and all the love songs made since,
all because your lips touched mine

I've realized
I'm a candle
without a flame
A book without pages
A sky without stars
And nothing
without you

I love her
I love her because
she steals my t shirts from my closest.
I love her because they are clearly too big for her.
I love her because when I catch her in it
the shoulder seams are down by her biceps but she
doesn't care.
I love her because she wears them to bed only to
wake up with her messy bun and my oversized t shirt.
I love her

If the world were to end tomorrow,
I think I'd be okay
stuck in this Paris café
consumed by the thought of you

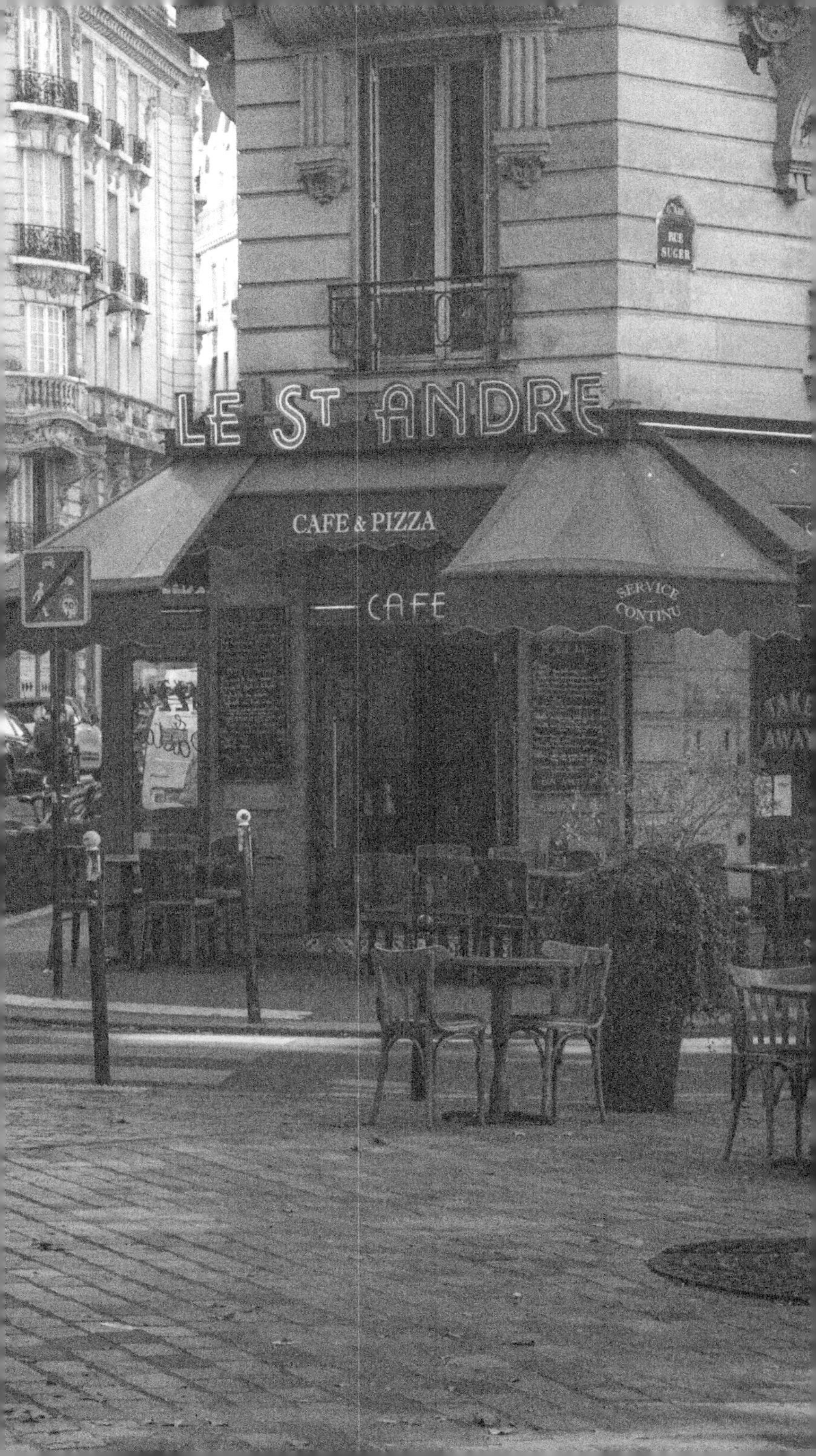
LE St ANDRE
CAFE & PIZZA
CAFE
SERVICE CONTINU
RUE SUGER

Even after all this time
You still make all the
butterflies in my
stomach take flight

You make me feel loved
You make me feel understood
And i hope you know
that you my dear
deserve all of this in return

"Do you trust me?"
He whispered
As his fingertips ran lightly alongside her
cami strap that sat loosely on her shoulder.

"Yes"
she replied

As she let him shed her of her clothing.
And with each piece falling to the floor so
did all her worries that she carried so heavily
on her mind.

I hope you know that when you hear me say:

- *get home safe*
- *have a good day*
- *feel better*
- *I hope you sleep well*

What I'm really saying is,
I love you
and it's stolen the meaning of other words

I would paint you
all the beautiful colors you radiate
your flesh be the canvas
my touch be my brush

YOU ARE ALL OF MY
FAVORITE PARTS OF MY
FAVORITE LOVE SONGS

to me
she is
5pm on a Friday in winter when
you leave work and finally take
that last turn around the corner to
your house
its where you see the beautiful
glow through the window
of a fire illuminating the living
room from the road.
She is the warm hug wrapped
around you tightly
as you're greeted when you walk
through the door
She to me will always
be home

The older you get, the more you realize that you don't want to be around drama, conflict, or stress. You just want a cozy home, good food, and to hang with the love of your life.

And just like the
leaves in autumn,
I fall for you
every time you
come around

And there was
something about you
I couldn't quite put
my finger on.
But whatever it was
it made me feel a
little more alive and
a far less lost

I will never be able to find the perfect
assortment of words to describe what you
mean to me. You are my world but even that
doesn't do justice.

When someone is able to
make you the happiest
person and the saddest
person at the same time,
that's when you know its real.
That's when you know you
have something worth loving.

I know you
like the back of my hand
and yet,
you still find a way to give me butterflies
as if we just met

THIS BED ISNT COMFORTABLE
WITHOUT YOU IN IT

When its my time to go
I hope they remember me.
I hope they remember me as the man who
wasn't afraid to live.
I hope they remember me as the man who
loved as much as I could.
Truly loved.
And the one I loved was you.

My favorite part
of the whole day
is getting to end it with you
because I get to fall asleep
and wake up to do it
all over again

Today I tried to explain to someone how you
make me feel but I couldn't put it into words.
I mean besides the obvious attraction:
your laugh, eyes, and dimples,
there are parts of you that I never knew existed.

For instance, the cute way you pretend to not
be asleep after you slowly start to drift, how
you constantly redecorate the décor around the
apartment just because, or how you never stop
trying to make those around you happy.

I couldn't explain that to someone in words, but
I think they knew when they saw me light up
just with the idea of thinking of you.

And I don't know where we'll be five years from
now, ten years or even thirty. I don't know if
we will be sitting on our porch swing watching
hummingbirds drink from the feeder, or if we
will be in the living room on our recliners with
our table trays watching our favorite show. But
what I do know is that wherever I am, whatever
I'm doing. I hope you're there with me.

A room
full of people
without you,
is an empty room

Tell me
everything you
hate about yourself,
so I know where
to pour a little
extra love into.

I wonder how many times
the author of my story had to
erase sentences, paragraphs
or even chapters until they
got it right, until they led me
to you.

and here I am
tangled up
in the sound of your heartbeat
and if this is what love is
I don't want anything else

I'm captivated by your lips,
the gentle curve they make
when you smile
But mostly, I'm captivated
by your lips
because they fit so
perfectly around mine.

She is
and forever will be
the perfect blend
of magic, chaos and poetry

and just like morning coffee
i'll always need you
to get though my day

happiness
looks so good on you darlin'

I didn't quite understand it,
It was like I was being pulled to you, bonded
by a simple touch of the hand like an
electromagnetic force.
I guess what I'm trying to say is all my
atoms love your atoms

my darling,
you will never hear me say
that I desire to fix you
for that would mean
that I think you are broken.
And you can show me
all your scars from battles
you do not speak of
in which you thought you'd lost,
and all the monsters that have walked
all over your heart.
And I will choose to remind you
that with all the worlds burden you carry
you still choose to love
and that makes you the furthest thing
from broken
for you are becoming.

I would sit in traffic on
any highway,
hang out in the waiting
room at the doctor's office,
or count each individual
grain of sand
on the beach,
whatever it took to slow
down time with you

beau·ti·ful
[byoodefel]

adjective
Definition: the person reading this

I hope you find someone who understands your love language. Someone who matches your effort. Someone who challenges you on all levels mentally and spiritually. But of all, I hope you find all these things in yourself first so you can be ready for this type of love.

On the days
where it's far too quiet in my head,
I need you to love me loudly

All she needs is good music, neck kisses,
coffee dates and midnight car rides with you

find the person
you want to
never stop
making
memories
with

My lips needed you,
longed for you,
craved you
like rain
in a drought

Do you want to know when I like you most?
Its not when everything is going your way and
things are all put together.
I like you most when you're overcoming
obstacles that bring your discomfort; in those
moments, that's when you teach me how to be
strong. I like you most on Sunday
mornings when you're in sweatpants from the
night before and your hair all in a mess, for
that's when you teach me to be
comfortable in my natural state.
I like you most when its 2am and we cant sleep
so we talk about the universe and all the things
we fear; that's when you show me how to let my
walls come down.

I don't like you most when you're perfect
I like you most you're real.

EVERYONE
DESERVES
A
LOVE
LIKE
YOURS

And the boy told the girl
*"don't be so focused on old pain that you
miss out on new love"*

& just like breathing,
loving you
is the easiest thing to do

Wake up at 5AM with me
when the rest of the world is still
sleeping. We can drive nowhere and buy
random flavored coffees.
We can drink them on the hood of my
car and try to guess the flavors from the
taste of each others lips.
Wake up at 5AM with me to see the
moon say hello to the sun.
We can take photos of the purple and
pink sky and stay quiet until the world isn't.

If you have to measure self-worth by a number
i hope you measure it in the number of times
you cried from laughing
with the ones who mean most to you

I barely knew you.
I barely knew the sound of your voice
or the way it felt when you touched me
but I fell in love with you.
It's one of those things you can quite put
into words.
I just knew the moment you came into
eyesight that you had this rare spark about
you. And I know rare things can't be
ignored so I fell in love with you because
everything in the universe told me to.

MY LIFE WILL END
AND SO WILL YOURS
SO JUST KISS ME ANYTIME

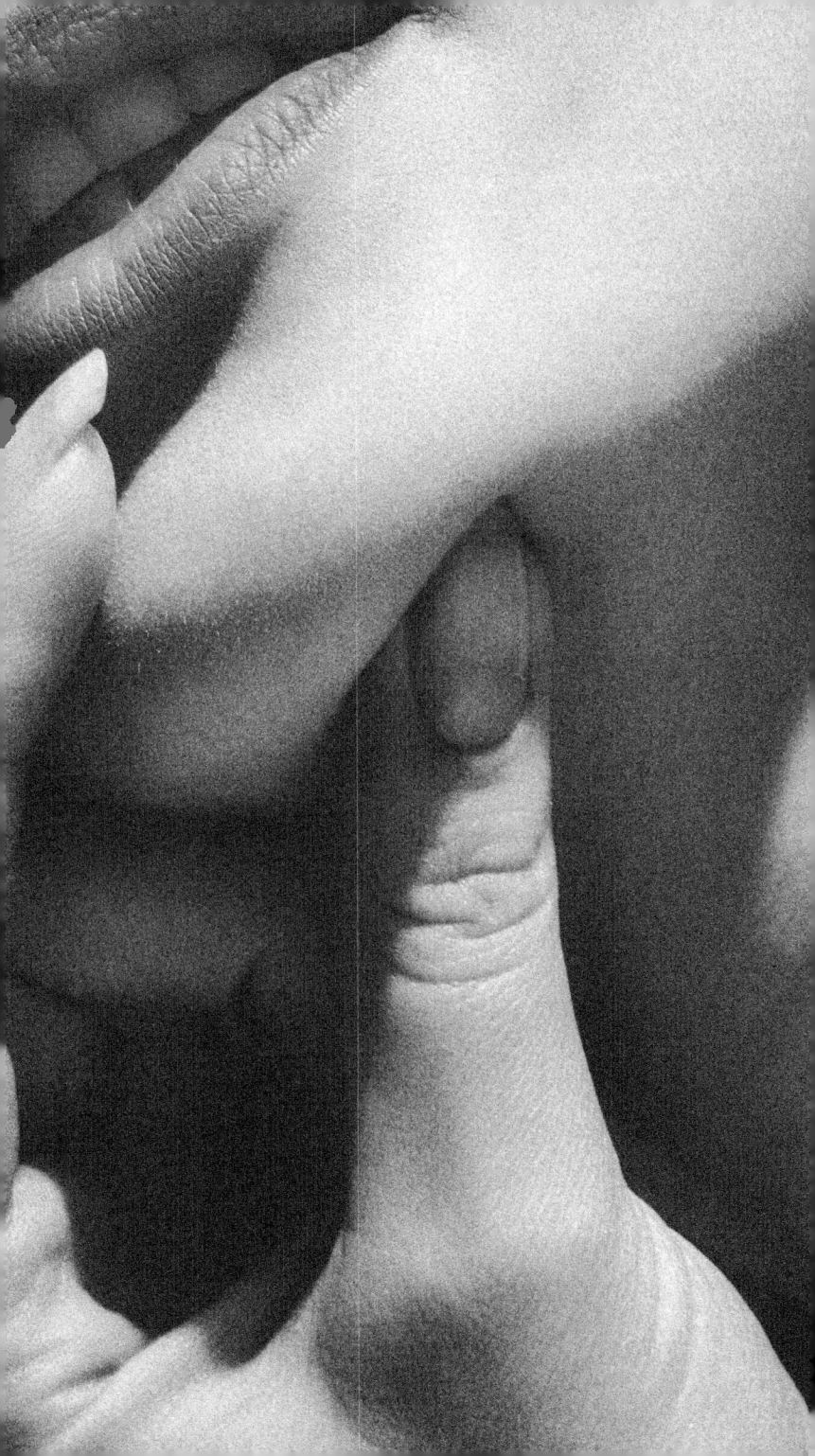

Life is too short for shitty sex and bad energy. So go be with someone who can fuck you right and treat you better

The moment you walked into my life, my
heart started to beat differently

I Hope You Know
Just How Better My Life Is
By You Being In It

Every inch of your body
could be tightly pressed up against mine
and i'd still want to pull you closer

It was when we were on the
couch talking in silly accents
for no reason at all.
It was when you called me
for the first time to just to
say you missed me.
It was when I saw you come
alive at your favorite
band's concert.
It was in all of our
moments that I knew I
wanted to make you laugh
for the rest of your life.

You deserve someone who'll take you to cute cafes for breakfast dates and buy you your favorite coffee.

Someone who'll give you back massages and play with your hair when you're both tangled up together on the couch.

Someone you can sit with and talk about big ideas and life with.

Someone who never fails to remind you that you're something special, someone worthy of being loved endlessly.

Yeah, someone should do all of this for you Because you shouldn't settle for anything less.

Your love was a symphony,
A perfect arrangement of notes
For those who were willing to listen
And I couldn't help but tap my foot

I'd be lying if I said I wasn't jealous,
i'm jealous of the breeze for it gets to crash into you,
i'm jealous of the dress for the way it hugs your hips,
and i'm jealous of the morning sun for it gets to kiss
your bare shoulders before I.

If love is a flame,
my love for you
is the sun

Do you ever crave someone?
Not for sex but for their
touch, their voice, their kiss,
their presence?

It's clear to me
that no matter where you roam
you always seem to have
a permanent place to stay
tucked away
in the corner of my mind
and just like a lighthouse
i'll always leave the light on
to guide you home

Come sit next to me
and let your warmth
melt all the cold I
carry inside me

you're like a book
i never want to finish
let me linger
in your pages
for a little bit
longer than forever
learning more and
more about you
as i read on

The exact moment I met you
I knew there was something special
about you,
something that I needed in my life.
It turns out that it wasn't a certain thing,
it was simply just you I needed.

please know that
you are a beautiful piece of art
and you have always been art
even before they came into the picture
and you'll continue to be art
if they ever decide to leave

The best part of your life
will be in those small moments.
The ones you don't even know you're in,
it's the nameless moments
the ones you spend
with someone who means
everything to you.

And maybe
i'll never be
able to find
the words to
describe just
how much
you mean to
me, but i'll
spend the rest
of my life
trying

I find it terrifying
yet strangely beautiful
that humans can attach themselves
to another soul
and not have the strength to let go

YOUR HEART
IS THE MOST BEAUTIFUL THING
ABOUT YOU

The boy asked the old man:
    "how do you know you love her?

The old man replied:
    "it's like you can't breathe when she walks
in the room because no matter how long you've
been together, she still finds ways to take your
breath away and you rush to kiss her so you can
steal just an ounce of air from her lungs"

The boy then asked timidly:
    "but what if it all falls apart?

The old man replied:
    "what if it all falls together?"

Printed in Great Britain
by Amazon